DAY TRADING STRATEGIES FOR BEGINNERS

THE COMPLETE GUIDE TO INVEST IN CRYPTOCURRENCY, BITCOINS, LITE-COINS, AND MAKE PROFIT ON THE STOCK MARKET

MAURY SWING

TABLE OF CONTENTS

INTRODUCTION 5

CHAPTER - 1
Day Trading: How It Works 13

CHAPTER - 2
Day Trading Vs. Swing Trading 19

CHAPTER - 3
Risk Management 25

CHAPTER - 4
Significance of Day Trading In
the Stock Market 35

CHAPTER - 5
Which Platform to Follow
When Investing 45

CHAPTER - 6
Strategies 55

CHAPTER - 7
Steps to Success on Trading 65

CHAPTER - 8
Rules of Day Trading 75

CHAPTER - 9
Beginners Traders 85

CHAPTER - 10
Huge Mistakes That Beginners Make 93

CHAPTER - 11
Tips for Day Trading In Options 101

CONCLUSION 109

INTRODUCTION

All over the world, stock markets open in the morning. Those day traders who think they can start trading while munching on their breakfast, with no preparation, are among those who make losses. All businesses open in the morning. No successful businessman just gets up, yawns and starts his business activities. Successful professionals arrive in their office with a clear idea of how they will tackle the work and related challenges. Likewise, to succeed in day trading, one must prepare beforehand. These preparations include many aspects; such as mental, physical, emotional, and financial.

Professional traders have clear advice for day traders; never trade if you are tired or stressed; never trade if you are feeling highly emotional, and trade with clear money management concepts. Day trading is a sophisticated business activity, where people try to earn money by using their intelligence. Therefore, physical or emotional stress can cause harm to your trading business. You will not be able to make rational decisions if you are tired or feeling stressed.

Before you start the day's trading, you should be physically, mentally and emotionally alert. A good night's sleep is necessary for traders to tackle the roller coaster ride of stock markets. Here are a few steps that will help you prepare for day trading with a cool temperament and calm mind.

Before going to sleep, keep your trading plan ready. Check the stock chart; make notes on the chart what big patterns the price created in the previous session. Note down the important support and resistance levels. Then mentally go over this chart and imagine how you will trade in the next session, in different trend conditions.

Do not spend too much time watching the news about stock markets or anything else. Watching the news may create doubts in your mind about stock trends and influence your decision-making power for the next session. If possible, do some breathing exercises or meditation before going to sleep, which will sharpen your focusing power and reduce stress.

Also, prepare your money-plans for the next trading session. How much will you invest? What will be your loss tolerance level? And, what will be your profit booking point? During the trading hours, these decisions have to be made in a split second, and if you are already prepared, you will not hesitate to make the right decision. These will also help you set your goals for intraday trading. Just stick to your goals and you will not face any decision-making problems during the trading hours.

The final stage of your preparation will be an hour before the markets open in the morning. This is the time when you check the news reports about the business and financial world, and the economic calendar. By doing so, you will know what events could influence that day's trading pattern in the stock market. You can also check how the world markets are trading in that session. Sometimes all markets trade in one direction, which will be beneficial to know before your local stock markets open.

Planning for Trading

In day trading, financial instruments are bought and sold within the same session. Sometimes more than once through the same day, to be successful in this endeavor, traders need to know where the price might make important moves. Technical charts are very helpful tools in deciphering this price moment. Anybody involved in stock trading relies heavily on stock charts, which is why successful traders always create their trading plans before making any trading decisions.

When you create a trading plan, you are creating an 'assistant' to help you during the trading hours. This assistant will have all the information you will need for day trading; such as trade entry, trade exit, profit booking, stop loss and major price moments. Nobody goes looking for a treasure trove without any map. Likewise; no trader worth his or her salt will trade without a trading plan. Let us look at how a trading plan is created:

A trading plan is based on research, takes time, but saves a lot of effort and precious money during the trading hours. It is one of the essential tools required for success in day trading. Every day trader has heard this saying 'fail to plan and plan to fail'. Professional traders don't tire of emphasizing the importance of a trading plan. If you take their advice and prepare a trading plan before the markets open, you are halfway through to successful trading.

A trading plan is prepared before markets open and so, it is open to revisions and changes after markets start to trade and price changes. Every trader has a different trading style and based on that his trading plan could differ from others. But every trading plan must have a few essential details. These are:

1. Major support and resistance levels: One must mark the major support and resistance levels on the trading chart because these will symbolize the trade entry and exit points. These levels should be visible on charts to help in decision making during the chaotic trading hours.

2. Trade entry rules: Your trading plan should include when and why you will enter a trade. This could be a detailed explanation like 'if the price goes above X level, then buy'. Or it could be just a green arrow pointing to that price level.

3. Trade exit rules: Like the trade entry point, mark a trade exit or profit booking points on your trading plan. You must follow these rules meticulously, otherwise, these will become useless, if you plan and do not follow them.

4. Money management rules: Some traders like to note down on their trading plan, how much money they will invest in the next session. They keep checking their profits and losses through the session, and if the day's loss reaches its threshold; they stop trading. This is a good example of money discipline while trading because, in the excitement of trading, one can lose sight of what is happening with the investment capital.

These are the most basic rules to include in the trading plan. As you gain experience and get a hold of trading patterns in stock markets, you can expand your trading plans and include more trading rules in it. But always remember, these rules must be followed. A trading plan is based on research about markets, so every rule is important. Breaking any rule will be like going against the market, which is always harmful to any trader.

Chart Reading & Candlestick Charts

Day traders use different charts for technical analysis. The main types are line charts, bar charts, and candlestick charts. Some Forex traders also use Heiken Ashi and Ranko charts, but candlestick charts remain the most favorite of traders. The reason for this popularity is its simplicity. A green candlestick shows a positive price movement and a red candlestick signals a fall in price. Day traders use various candlestick patterns to decipher the market trend.

The candlestick charts are more than a hundred years old. These were first used by Japanese rice traders to document the rise and fall in the rice prices. It was such an accurate system that stock traders also adopted it and it has since been a popular chart creating tool.

A single candlestick has two main parts; a body and a tail or wick. The body of the candlestick shows the opening and closing levels, while the wick shows the high and low marks. A green body shows that the price opened low but closed higher. And a red body shows higher open, but lower closing in that time frame. A single candlestick can be assigned to different time frames, ranging from one second to one month. These candlesticks make various patterns on charts. Traders try to decipher the price moment by how long the wick, or the body is, and how every candlestick is placed with other nearby candlesticks.

Candlestick charts are also used for automatic or algorithm trading, where buy and sell signals are generated by various patterns formed by candlesticks.

The up and down movement in stock prices creates candlesticks on charts. Sometimes, a single candlestick can indicate a trend reversal from high to low or low to high. These are called engulfing candlesticks and are so large that they completely engulf the previous candlestick. These can be both bullish and bearish candlesticks. A bullish candlestick is formed when the price-move creates a big positive or green candlestick, which overshadows the previous one. It signals that the price is ready to move higher and to start an uptrend.

Its opposite is a bearish engulfing candlestick pattern. Here, the stock price makes a big red candlestick overshadowing the previous one. This signals big selling pressure and shows that the price will fall further.

Another popular form of a candlestick is "Doji". Usually, this candlestick forms near the top or the bottom, after the price has made a long moment in either direction. In a Doji candlestick, the body is tiny, and the wicks are long. A small body denotes uncertainty in buyers and sellers; which shows that the market cannot decide whether to go up or down. Such an uncertain signal on top may indicate a trend reversal, and traders prepare for a fall in the market. A Doji formation at the bottom signals that the downtrend may come to an end and traders look for confirmation of a price-rise from lower levels.

Candlesticks create many types of patterns on a technical chart. This could involve a single or two or more candlesticks. There are many books about candlesticks and how to read candlestick charts. Traders who wish to know more about these charts, can read some of those books and enhance their knowledge.

CHAPTER - 1

Day Trading: How It Works

How Day Trading Works

Once you start day trading, you can use a myriad number of techniques and methods to execute trades. For example, you can choose to trade based solely on your "gut feeling" or you can go to the other extreme of relying entirely on mathematical models that optimize trading success through elaborate automated trading systems.

Regardless of the method, you can have limitless day-trading profit potential once you master day trading. Here are some of the strategies many expert day traders use profitably.

One is what's called "trading the news", which is one of the most popular day trading strategies since time immemorial. As you may have already gleaned from the name, it involves acting upon any press-released information such as economic data, interest rates, and corporate earnings.

Another popular day trading strategy is called "fading the gap at the open". This one's applicable on trading days when a security's price opens with a gap, i.e., below the previous day's lowest price or above the previous day's highest price.

"Fading the gap at the open" means taking an opposite position from the gap's direction. If the price opens with a downward gap, i.e., below the previous day's lowest price, you buy the security, if the price opens with an upward gap, i.e., it opens higher than the previous day's highest price, you short or sell the security.

There was a time when the only people able to trade in financial markets were those working for trading houses, brokerages, and financial institutions. The rise of the internet, however, made things easier for individual traders to get in on the action. Day Trading, in particular, can be a very profitable career, as long as one goes about it in the right way.

However, it can be quite challenging for new traders, especially those who lack a good strategy. Furthermore, even the most experienced day traders hit rough patches occasionally. As stated earlier, Day Trading is the purchase and sale of an asset within a single trading day. It can happen in any marketplace, but it is more common in the stock and forex markets.

Day traders use short-term trading strategies and a high level of leverage to take advantage of small price movements in highly liquid currencies or stocks. Experienced day traders have their finger on events that lead to short-term price movements, such as the news, corporate earnings, economic statistics, and interest rates, which are subject to market psychology and market expectations.

When the market exceeds or fails to meet those expectations, it causes unexpected, significant moves that can benefit attuned day traders. However, venturing into this line of business is not a decision prospective day trader should take lightly. It is possible for day traders to make a comfortable living trading for a few hours each day.

However, for new traders, this kind of success takes time. Think like several months or more than a year. For most day traders, the first year is quite tough. It is full of numerous wins and losses, which can stretch anyone's nerves to the limit. Therefore, a day trader's first realistic goal should be to hold on to his/her trading capital.

Volatility is the name of the game when it comes to Day Trading. Traders rely on a market or stock's fluctuations to make money. They prefer stocks that bounce around several times a day, but do not care about the reason for those price fluctuations. Day traders will also go for stocks with high liquidity, which will allow them to enter and exit positions without affecting the price of the stock.

Day traders might short sell a stock if its price is decreasing or purchase if it is increasing. Actually, they might trade it several times in a day, purchasing it and short-selling it a number of times, based on the changing market sentiment. In spite of the trading strategy used, their wish is for the stock price to move.

Day Trading, however, is tricky for two main reasons. Firstly, day traders often compete with professionals, and secondly, they tend to have psychological biases that complicate the trading process.

Professional day traders understand the traps and tricks of this form of trading. In addition, they leverage personal connections, trading data subscriptions, and state-of-the-art technology to succeed. However, they still make losing trades. Some of these professionals are high-frequency traders whose aim is to skim pennies off every trade.

The Day Trading field is a crowded playground, which is why professional day traders love the participation of inexperienced traders. Essentially, it helps them make more money. In addition, retail traders tend to hold on to losing trades too long and sell winning trades too early.

Due to the urge to close a profitable trade to make some money, retail investors sort of pick the flowers and water the weeds. In other words, they have a strong aversion to making even a small loss. This tends to tie their hands behind their backs when it comes to purchasing a declining asset. This is due to the fear that it might decline further.

CHAPTER - 2

Day Trading Vs. Swing Trading

Day Trading vs. Swing Trading

Day trading is similar to swing trading in certain aspects. The major difference between the two is that trades entered in day trading are closed that very same day. Trades usually last only a couple of hours, and sometimes, even minutes. This is totally different from swing trading where trades can last for days, weeks, and sometimes, even longer.

Swing trading requires less time on the trading platforms compared to day trading. You do not need to sit down all day observing your screen and noting all the tiny movements that occur during the day. Day traders can hardly afford to leave the trading platform as they risk losing money.

As a swing trader, you are able to maximize profitability in the short-term by benefiting from most of the market swings. You can also rely solely on technical analysis to carry out trades and still be profitable.

The only major challenge when it comes to day trading is that you can be exposed to unexpected risks on the weekends or overnight. This is likely to happen when major events or announcements are made that can affect stock price movement. You can sometimes lose money on your trades when there is an abrupt or unexpected market reversal. And, sometimes, you may lose out big time on long-term opportunities by pursuing pretty short-term trends.

In essence, day trading and swing trading are very similar in some respects. The major difference is the holding time. The minimum holding time with swing trading is overnight while day traders have to close out their trades before the expiry of the trading session. Positions are always limited to a day.

When a position is held overnight, certain things can happen. For instance, the trend could head downwards, or the position could suffer risks like gaps. Both day and swing traders have access to trading margins from their brokers. A margin is simply a loan granted by the broker to clients for purposes of enhancing trades. Swing traders have access to about 50% leverage which means that a trader can receive a loan of up to 50% from the broker.

The definition of day trading, which includes day traders keep their shares for the day. His posit they close their positions at the end of each day, and again the next day. On the other hand, they have swing trader bonuses for days and sometimes even months; Investors are sometimes left for years. The short-term nature of the trading day reduced some risks because nothing can happen overnight, causing significant losses. At the same time, many other types of investors to go to bed thinking that his position is in perfect condition to wake up the next morning and discovered that the company announced huge profits or CEO is accused of fraud.

But there is another side not always a disadvantage, right? Select the values and positions that have to work a day trader or the day is done. Tomorrow does not exist for a given office. Meanwhile, swing trader or investor has the luxury of time, as it may take some time to get into the role they should. In the long run, markets are practical and efficient, and the prices reflect all information on the link. Sorry, we can

Take a few days to realize efficiency.

Day traders are speculators, who work in a zero-sum market one day at a time. This makes the dynamics of various other types of financial activities that you can participate in. On the business rules, adoption day to help choose a good deed or to find significant investment funds in recent years are no longer used. Day Trading is a different game with different rules.

They speculate, do not cover the professional players are divided into two categories: hedgers and speculators. Speculators were looking to take advantage of price changes. Arbitrageurs try to protect themselves against price changes. They ensure that your choice of buying and selling are safe and cannot win. Therefore, select the elements that offset their exposure to another market.

For example, the cover should be considered as a food, a farmer who creates or increases the ingredients that the company needs. The Company may seek to hedge against the risk of rising prices of elemental components - like corn, oil, and meat - purchase agreements with these ingredients. Therefore, if rates rise, corporate profits in contracts to help finance the rising costs will have to pay for these ingredients. If prices remain the same or fall, the company loses the contract price, which is the compensation for the company. Corn producer, soybeans, or farm

Secondly, it is beneficial if prices rise and suffer if they fall. To protect against falling prices, the farmer can sell futures contracts on these products. Their futures position to make money if the price dropped to compensate for a decrease in their products. And if rates rose, losing money on contracts, but the increase in its harvest offsets this loss.

The commodity markets were designed to help farmers manage risk and find buyers for their products. The equity and bond markets were created to encourage investors to finance businesses. Almost immediately, rumors ran in all these markets, but it was not his primary goal.

Day traders are speculators. They try to make money in the market as they are now. They manage risk by spreading wealth carefully, using stop orders and limit orders positions predetermined price levels were reached as quickly as possible in the vicinity and the sunset. Day traders do not manage risk by offsetting their place in the same way as the insurer. They use other techniques to reduce losses, such as money management with caution and stop and limit orders.

CHAPTER – 3

Risk Management

Managing the risk helps to cut losses. It can also help to protect an account of a trader from losing all his or her money. The chance arrives while the trader is facing a loss. The dealer will expose him or herself to make profits in the business whether it can be handled. A key but often prerequisite overlooked for active trading successfully is this.

After all, without a proper risk management strategy, substantial profits generated by the trader might be lost entirelyby1-2 bad trades. And how can you figure out the right strategies to reduce industry risks? This book will discuss a few strategies that might be used for the protection of the profit of trading of yours.

KEY POINTS

• Trading is sometimes thrilling and even lucrative if you can remain centered, due diligence should be conducted and hold at bay your emotions.

• However, successful traders ought to implement risk reduction strategies so that risks will not get out of sight.

• It's a wise way to remain in the position and take a pragmatic and rational approach to reduce costs by stop requests, benefit sharing and defensive puts.

Trades Planning

As the famous Sun Tzu (general of Chinese military) said: A fight is already won before it begins or fought in real. This statement means that strategy and planning — battles don't — win the wars. Successful traders similarly, often the phrase is quoted: "Planning the trade strategy and trade planning strategy." As the planning in war, for the future can often be meant the in-between difference of failure and success.

First, try to ensure that right is the broker to trade frequently. Any brokers work for clients who never deal. High commissions are charged by them and do not offer active traders the proper analytical tools.

S / L (Stop-loss) and T / P (Take-Profit) points are two main forms traders should schedule accordingly as they sell. Effective merchants know the amount they want to offer and the level they are able to sell at. They will then calculate the subsequent product probability against returns that can meet the goals of them. If a sufficiently high adjusted return is they carry out the trade.

In comparison, ineffective trader frequently joins a deal without getting some knowledge of points from which they would be selling at some profit or loss. Similarly as gamblers on some streak lucky — or unlucky — emotions start taking control and dictating trades of them. Losses also encourage investors to hang on and wait to regain their capital, whilst losses will trigger traders to keep on imprudently for even greater rewards.

Adopt the Rule of One-Percent

Many day traders are adopting what is considered the one percent law. Basically, this thumb law indicates you can never involve more than one percent of your money or trading portfolio in a single transaction. And if 10,000 dollars in the trading account you have, there will be no more than 100 dollars in your place on any given instrument.

This technique is popular with traders with accounts below 100,000 dollars—some also go up to 2 percent if they might manage it. A lot of traders with higher balances in their accounts can choose a low percentage to go because when your account rises in size, so does your place. The easiest strategy to hold your risks in control is to maintain the limit below 2 percent — any higher and you'd damage the trading account to a significant sum.

How to use Stop Loss& Have Points of Profit

A point of stop-loss is the amount a seller would be selling a product and have a trade loss. This also occurs when a trader wished for a deal will not work out.

These points are built to resist the mindset of "it'll come back" and reduce losses until they increase. For starters, if the stock falls below a main level of support, the traders always sell as early as possible. Similarly On the other side, the price of stock selling by the trader and have a trading profit is a take-off point. That is when, given the risks, the upside additional one is limited. For instance, towards an important resistance level stock is approaching after a big upward move, traders might want to sell before the occurring a consolidation period.

Measures Set Points of Stop-Loss More Effectively

The setting of the stop-loss and taking points of the profit is mostly achieved using quantitative analysis, but a crucial function in timing may also be played through conceptual analysis. For instance, a trader if keeps ahead stock then the earnings as anticipation rises, he/she will decide to sell until the news reaches the market because expectations have risen too big, regardless the profit-taking price has reached.

The best way for these points setting is by moving averages, as their calculation is easy and by the market tracked widely. The five, nine, twenty, fifty, hundred, and two hundred-day averages are key moving averages. These averages are better calculated by adding them to the chart of the market and deciding if the price of the stock has, in the previous time, responded to them as a degree of encouragement or resistance.

Another best way to stop-loss position or take levels of profit is on trend lines of resistance or support. This may be derived by comparing previous peaks or lows which existed at a large amount above normal. As with averages moving, the aim is to decide the rate when the price can respond to the lines of trend and the high volume of course. When these points are set, some important considerations are as follows:

- Use the moving averages of longer-term for

more risky stocks to popular the probability of a pointless market change causing order of stop-loss. Moving averages change to suit goal price points.

- Longer goals, for example, can use larger rolling averages for reducing the number of produced signals.

- Stop losses will not be similar to the existing volatility range high-to-low than 1.5 times because they are more likely to be performed without justification.

- The stop loss is adjusted accordingly to the volatility of the market. If the price of the stock doesn't move a lot then it can tighten the points of stop-loss.

- Using recognized simple events like earnings reports as main moments to be in the trade or out as the volatility and confusion can increase.

How to Calculate Expected Return

It is also necessary to set stop-loss and profit points taken up for expected returns calculations. The value of this measure cannot be overestimated as it allows traders to consider and rationalize about their trades. This also offers them a structured means of evaluating different trades and only selecting the best successful ones. By following formula calculation can be done:

[(Gain Probability) x (Take Profit percent Gain)] + [(Loss Probability) x (Stop-Loss percent Loss)]

This result consequence is a return expected on the successful investor, and then it will weigh by the investor against other incentives to decide the stocks to sell. The gain/loss probability can also be calculated by the historical breakout's usage and support breakdowns or trader's resistance — or by the educated guess for experienced traders.

Diversification and Hedging

Be sure you get the most out of your trade means you never put the eggs in a single basket. If all of the money of yours is put into a single stock or instrument, prepare yourself for a huge loss. So, always diversify the investments of yours — in both industry and market capitalization, also the geographic of the market. This not only lets you control the exposure but it opens up also further doors for you.

You also may find yourself having to hedge the position of yours when you need to. When due the results consider a stock position. Using options you can take the contrasting position that might help you in your position protection. The hedge will then be unwinded as market behavior subsides.

Put Options Downside

If licensed you are for the options trading, you can also use the buying of a put option downside, also called as a defensive put, as a protection to prevent losses from some deal that changes sour. The put option grants you the opportunity, not the duty to offer the stock underlying at or until expires the option at a defined date. So, if you purchase XYZ stock at 100 dollars and the 80 dollars 6-month premium is bought for one dollar per contract, you would be essentially protected from any market decline below 79 dollars (80 dollars strike less the 1 dollar paid premium).

Bottom Line

It should always be known by the traders, before executing, when they decide or plan for entering or exiting a trade. By effectively stop losses using, a trader can reduce or decrease losses not only but also needlessly a trade is being exited for several times. In conclusion, plan your battle ahead of the time so you will know you've already achieved the goal. As people start aging, they usually face health risks more. Pure risk assessment includes the method of defining, analyzing, and controlling these threats – a proactive tactic to plan for the unpredictable. The basic risk management methods are avoidance, sharing, retention transfer, and reduction and prevention of losses – to all facets can apply to the life of an individual and can pay over the long term.

Here's a glance at all five approaches and how they can be extended to safety risk reduction.

1. Avoidance

This is a tool for reducing liability by avoiding engaging in behaviors that may cause harm, illness, or death. Cigarette smoking example of such operation because stopping it will reduce the safety and risk of finance.

Death leading cause in the United States is smoking and around 480,000 lives in a year it claims, according to the American Lung Association.1 Additionally, the United States Centers for Controlling Disease& Prevention states that the number one factor for lung cancer is smoking and the incidence rises more the more individuals consume.

Life insurance providers reduce this danger by increasing smokers' rates than non-smokers on their edge. Based on geography, family size, age, and status of smoking, insurance insurers are eligible to raise rates under the Universal Health Care Act, commonly known as Obama treatment. A premium surcharge of up to 50 percent for smokers is allowed by the law.

2. Retention

It is the recognition and understanding of a program as given. This risk is usually a help cost to offset bigger risks, like choosing health insurance lower premium plans that have a deductible rate higher. The cost of paying more medical expenses out of pocket is the initial risk of when health problems arise. When the condition is very serious or dangerous for life than there are additional care plans offered that offset much of the expenses above the penalty. If the patient does not have significant health conditions that require any extra insurance costs for a year, instead they prevent extra expenditures, thus reducing the greater danger.

3. Sharing

Shared risk is also enforced by benefits employer-based which allows the business to pay the employee an insurance premiums portion. Essentially, that spreads the responsibility with the health services provider and other workers involved in it. The premium cost must proportionately shrink with more participants sharing the risks is understanding. Individuals can consider it in the best interest of them to engage in risk sharing by choosing health insurance and insurance of life policies for employees, where appropriate.

CHAPTER – 4

Significance of Day Trading In the Stock Market

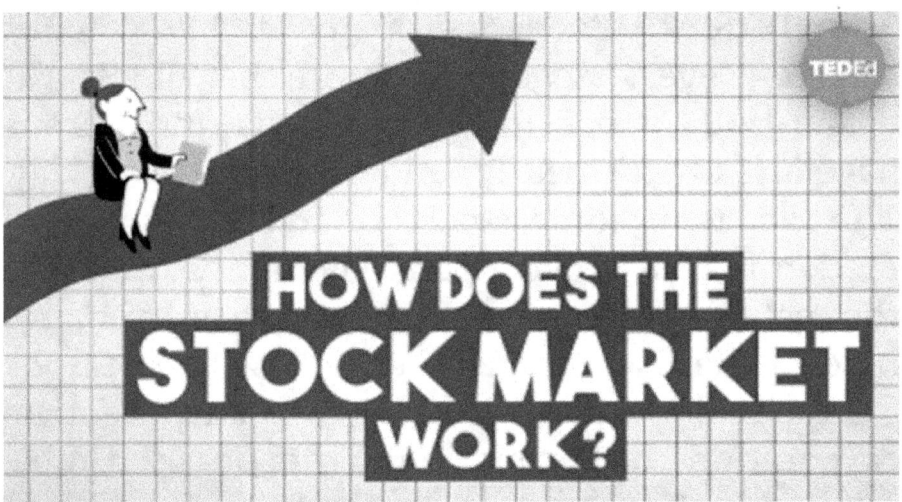

HOW DOES THE STOCK MARKET WORK?

Effects of Stock Market on Day Trading

A variety of factors may influence the entry (buy) of an investor into or exit (sell) from a given stock or market. The value of scheduling the entry (buy) will vary depending on the investor and his or her priorities and timetable for investing. The tinier the time span, of course, the more important the entry is; unique entries matter little to long-term depositors.

That being said, all investors should be conscious of some of the more popular moving market forces that can disturb the price of a stock. In being aware of these business subtleties, buyers will make better investments and, in return, capture an extra or two percent. Let's look at the eight variables that can have a significant effect on the typical trading day.

Foreign Market Place

The NY Stock Exchange opens at 9:30 am for exchange every single day. Before the "Big Board" opens trade, stock markets in Asia and Europe have already (or nearly) ended their trading day. The fact is, if some stocks or industries have a predominantly good or poor day in those markets, the Feeling could have a consequence on exchange here in the U.S. For instance, a negative outlook for technology firms in Asia or pharmaceutical corporations in Europe could effortlessly tumble over into U.S. trading and trigger American technology and pharmaceutical shares to take a descent.

This, in fact, has considerable adverse effects on all the big indexes. When you see big negative activity impacting your segment in a foreign market, it may be healthier to wait until the dust relaxes before you get into place. This would save some of your money right from the beginning.

Financial Data

If around is talk of China being able to reevaluate its currency (the Yuan), then it will cause outside exporters to China to trade higher stocks of exporters. (The reasoning behind that is that more U.S. - made goods with a higher Yuan would be available to Chinese companies and individuals).

Parenthetically, increases in interest rates may also cause liquidity to drift into or out of major markets. For instance, if U.K. interest rates Upsurge, investors can escape for healthier opportunities in that market. U.S. firms will often gain the benefit.

When you made your decision to invest, you should be mindful of any financial news that comes out or will come out when you go into your place. If a highly predicted economic release is about to surface that could result in market unpredictability, it may be paramount to wait for its announcement rather than jumping in early.

Futures Statistics

While a person may be prepared for securing or sell "available" stock at a sensible price, upcoming data may offer the individual a better indulgence of whether that would be possible in authenticity. Index futures represent the most significant market directories. They start interchange beforehand the stock marketplace and are a very decent pointer of what it will sense like to open up the stock market. This is for the reason that index futures values are closely connected to the actual point.

In short, depositors will search to see if futures indentures traded in premarket interchange are higher or lower. It would give them a stronger sense of where the directory they are looking might be shifting "after the break." Normally you would hear CNBC or other market sources reporting about DJIA or S&P 500 futures activity before they break.

Purchasing At the Opening

It may not be a good impression to purchase or sell stock at the opening of the market. Why?

Usually, a lot of purchasing and retailing occurs throughout the first hour of the interchange day. Essentially, the opening hour of exchange is the first time most market members have to join or leave the stock, and can easily produce higher than the regular capacity of trading. Many market members respond to the innumerable news items that seemed between the concluding of yesterday and the opening of today, containing major market news proceedings such as economic developments and political shifts.

A handful of bellwether inventories announce earnings or distribute news before the open. This can cause some depositors (both retail and institutional) to move wealth at the first chance they get in or out of a zone — creating crazy haste at the open.

Noontime Trading Pause

Usually, there is a reduction in trading (meaning the trade capacity) at noon because the majority of the big news proceedings are out of the marketplace. Stock values can also drop some ground during this break.

When this occurs, stocks can be bought at 1 pm at a low price than purchased at 11 am. It is significant to study once again because this can influence both admission points and departure points.

Analyst Assessments

An analyst can publicize an intraday memo that can disturb a given stock or subdivision significantly. As a landfill, do not overlook to check monetary websites or watch TV publicity videos. When a big company has either been promoted or downgraded, seek to determine the possible effect on certain markets and the economy as a whole.

For example, if a big stock of semiconductors is demoted by a well-known analyst due to slackening requests for goods from that firm, it would be fair to conclude that other smaller players would experience similar trends. It may also be rational to believe that stocks of computer makers (which buy large amounts of semiconductors) may also be affected.

Also, if a major homebuilder has been promoted due to strong requests for their homes, it is fair to believe that other big players in the industry (who have the same physical footprint) will experience similar requests increases. By definition, rising demand for new homes may mean a big opportunity for home development stores and furniture manufacturers.

Social Networking and Blogs

The internet has altered how people participate, as well as how the general community gets news; therefore, whether a web author or reporter spreads a bullish or bearish article about business throughout the day of exchange, it can have a major consequence on their stock.

All investors will endure to search the web and visit main news sites during the day to see if the public domain has any potentially market-moving news articles. Be vigilant about avoiding sites offering endorsements based on the shares they own. Such pump-and-dump schemes predominate on the network.

Friday Exchange

Even if you're a "buy and hold" investor, on Friday (usually in the afternoon), a minor number of trade and institutional traders normally settle their shares, so they don't have to keep their positions and take perils over the weekend. What do you mean by that?

This means that stocks during the last few hours of the trading day can and frequently sell-off Friday afternoon, if for no other cause than traders are looking to go home "square" (without positions on their books). Keep this in observance when trying to find an appropriate time to join or leave a stock place on Fridays.

Although company-specific incidents can impact stock prices, there are a variety of other variables that can also impact the shares. Savvy investors will know it.

What to Aspect for In a Day Exchange Stock

With thousands of stocks to select from, how will you determine which ones you will be concentrating on for day trading? Trying to find it out can get complicated. Every day, some traders discover new stocks to sell, or look for stocks that fall out of trend. Many watches for stocks that break out, or are the most unpredictable, of support or resistance rates.

Many traders are examining for increasingly unpredictable stocks, selling a few of such stocks for weeks on end. There are also those who merely regularly trade the same one or two stocks.

This last strategy is more advantageous to day traders as they are less research-intensive—day traders do not need to continuously locate new stocks, or check for instability and breakouts. When you are one of these traders and want to trade one or two stocks (or ETFs) on a constant basis, there are a few considerations that can help you determine which stocks to choose from.

Capacity

An active day trader needs an appropriate amount of stocks to enter and exit trades on request. The larger the number, the simpler it is with little to no slippage to enter and exit positions (relative to smaller number stocks). Slippage happens when the price of the sales order or stop-loss varies between the time the order is issued, and when the transaction occurs. This is usually in circumstances where orders are higher than the average number of a bid or offer shares.

Although tastes vary, traders on several days will exchange stocks with a regular amount of at least 1 million (often several million) trades. Some of the most widely traded securities in the U.S. are an exchange-traded fund (ETF)—the S&P 500 SPDR (SPY)—which has a steady capacity of about 95 million. A portfolio screener will help you narrow down the number of stocks to an amount that you can handle. If there are still plenty of stocks in the list, work to minimize them by just considering stocks in a regular average volume that do 3 million (or more).

Instability

A growing day-to-day trading approach is to trading stocks that are rapidly moving all day. Every stock has a different "personality" unpredictability. Some stocks will move around 0.5 percent per day on average, some move around 1 percent per day, and some stocks exchange more than 5 percent per day.

Whatever stocks you want to trade depends on your business style, reflexes, broker and personality. Most people find it tolerable to trade a stock that moves 0.5 percent to 2 percent per day while considering a stock's major swipes that move 5 percent per day difficult to deal with.

Many people are not mentally or bodily sufficiently supple to respond to a large number of unstable stocks and the price variations they may undergo. This will impede the successful execution of trades in stocks with higher instability.

To make it more manageable, a stock screener (such as Finviz) may be used to thin down the number of pillories to a size that's good for you. When after the reduction, there are still a lot of stocks on the list, seek to minimize the size of the list further by only bearing in mind stocks that shift in small amounts, such as 1 or 2 percent.

A few day traders can even opt to sell stocks on news that moves a stock significantly. Such are called impact stocks, which can deliver uncertainty as a competitive advantage.

Trend or Assortment

Other factors to ponder are the trend and assortment of investments. There are a variety of traders, trend traders and others who are effectively doing both. Scope refers to the difference between low and high prices of a stock in a given exchange period, though trend denotes the general way of the price of a stock. The prices may shift up or down uninterruptedly, suggesting an uptrend or downtrend.

A stock screener will help you classify trends or variety stocks and you'll still have a list of stocks to apply your daytime trading approaches. It will take some effort to find stocks that agree to your trading system, as the crescendos within stocks shift over time. However, time is well spent, since a technique implemented in the right context is far more successful.

CHAPTER - 5

Which Platform to Follow When Investing

The main tools you'll need for day trading are an online broker and an order execution platform. It goes without saying that you'll also need a very good internet connection and a computer on which to execute your trades on the platform. And if you're not part of a day trading community yet, you'll also need a stock scanner.

The Broker

You'll need a very good broker, who'll be your access to the securities market you plan to day trade in, e.g., the stock market. Take note that your broker can't just be good: it has to be very good. Why?

Since you can't access the stock market or other securities markets directly, you'll need to go through a broker. Even if you choose your SIPs correctly, you can still lose money in your trades if your broker's slow to execute your order at your target price or if their system suffers from frequent glitches.

It can be challenging to choose a broker because there are many of them out there. Some offer top service but are expensive while some charge very low fees but their service is crappy. Worse, some are both expensive and crappy! To help you narrow down your choices to quality brokers, I'll provide a list of really good ones at the end of this book in the appendix.

Minimum Equity Requirement

The United States Securities and Exchange Commission (SEC) and the Financial Industry Regulatory Authority (FINRA) enforce rules on people who day trade. They use the term Pattern Day Trader to qualify those who can engage in day trading with stock brokerage firms operating in the United States.

The qualify pattern day traders as those who day trades, i.e., takes and closes positions within the same day, at least four times in the last five business days. The SEC and FINRA require that pattern day traders must have a minimum equity balance of $25,000 in their brokerage account before they day trade. When the equity balance falls below this amount for one reason or another, brokers are compelled to prohibit pattern day traders from executing new day trades until they're able to bring their equity back up to at least $25,000.

Many newbie day traders, especially those who only have this minimum amount, look at this rule as more of a hindrance to day trading glory rather than a protective fence against day trading tragedies. They don't realize that it's mean to keep them from taking excessive day trading risks that can easily wipe out their trading capitals in a jiffy because of their brokers' commissions and fees.

While this rule is the minimum requirement under the law, many brokers and dealers may use a stricter definition of a pattern day trader for purposes of transacting with them. The best thing to do is to clarify this minimum equity requirement with your chosen broker to avoid confusion later on.

If you can't afford the $25,000 minimum equity requirement for day trading, you can opt to trade with an offshore broker instead. They're brokerage firms that operate outside the United States such as Capital Markets Elite Group Limited, which operates out of Trinidad and Tobago. Because these brokers operate outside the jurisdiction of FINRA, they're not subject to the pattern day trader rule. This means you're also not subject to the same minimum amount.

Direct-Access and Conventional Brokers

Conventional brokers normally reroute their customers' orders, including yours, to other firms through some sort of pre-agreed upon order processing scheme. Thus, executing your orders through conventional brokers involve more steps and can take significantly more time. And when it comes to day trading, speed is essential.

Conventional brokers are often referred to as full-service brokers because they tend to provide customers with other services such as market research and investment advice, among others. Because of these "extras", their commissions and fees are usually much higher than direct-access brokers. Conventional or full-service brokers are ideal for long-term investors and swing traders because they're not as particular with the speed of trade executions as day traders are.

Compared to full-service or conventional brokers, direct-access brokers focus more on the speed of trade executions than research and advisory services. And because they often skip the extra services to focus on providing fast and easy access to the stock market, they charge fewer commissions and fees. This has earned many of them the alias "discount brokers".

Direct-access brokers use very powerful computer programs and provide customers with online platforms through which they can directly trade the stock market, whether it's the NASDAQ or the NYSE. And while they provide the necessary trade execution speeds required in day trading, they're not perfect and they have their share of challenges.

One such challenge is the imposition of monthly trading volume quotas. If you fail to meet their minimum monthly trading volume, they'll charge you an "inactivity fee", which often serves as their minimum monthly commission from your and all their other clients' accounts. However, not all discount brokerage firms impose inactivity fees.

Another challenge particular to direct-access brokers concerns newbie day traders, i.e., familiarity with direct-access trading. With conventional brokers, all a newbie trader needs to do is tell their broker the details of their orders and the broker will be the one to take care of all things related to executing their orders in the market. With direct-access brokers, the day trader him or herself executes the orders through the broker's online platform or software.

This can be quite challenging for newbie day traders because apart from choosing their SIPs, they also need to know how to execute their orders on the platform properly. But since day trading is a more sophisticated form of stock market trading, the chances are high that newbie day traders have enough experience with direct-access trading already.

Trading Platform

A trading platform pertains to the computer program or software that you'll use to day trade. This is different from the direct-access broker itself, but many traders make the mistake of thinking they're one and the same.

The trading platform is what you'll use to send your orders to the stock exchange, which the direct-access broker will clear on your behalf. While it's different from the direct-access brokers, it's not unusual for such brokers to develop and have their clients use their own proprietary trading platforms to trade stocks in the exchange.

The number and quality of the features of trading platforms influence the price direct-access brokers charge their clients for their services. The more features a platform has, the higher the commissions and fees may be and vice versa.

A very important feature that you should look for in a trading platform is Hotkeys. Without them, you may not be able to execute trades fast enough to make them profitable. Considering that day trading focuses on stocks with relatively high volatility, being a second or two late can spell the difference of taking and closing positions at the ideal prices and missing out on profitable day trading opportunities.

Market Data

Unlike long-term investors and swing traders who only need end-of-day price data that's available for free online, day traders need real time data as the trading day unfolds because they need to get in and out of positions within a matter of hours, minutes, or even seconds. And unfortunately, access to real time intraday price data isn't free and you'll need to pay monthly fees to your direct-access broker or the platform owner (if different from the brokerage firm) for them. Just ask your direct-access broker for details on their monthly fees for access to real time day trading data.

Two of the most basic types of data that you'll need to look at as a day trader are the bid and ask prices. The bid prices are the prices at which other traders and investors are willing to buy a particular stock. The ask prices are the prices at which other traders and investors are willing to sell a particular stock.

The bid and ask prices are arranged such that the best price is at the top. The best bid price is the highest one, i.e., the best price for sellers is the highest price at which buyers are willing to buy. It's considered the best price from the perspective of buyers. Bid and ask prices also indicate the number of shares that other traders and investors are willing to buy or sell them at specific prices.

The bid prices are usually listed on the left side while the ask prices are usually listed on the right such that the best bid and ask prices are right beside each other. If you want to execute your buy orders immediately, you "buy up" the best ask price. If you want to immediately execute your sell orders, "sell down" at the best bid price.

Orders

The Day Trading Orders

The three most important types of day trading orders are market, limit, and marketable limit orders.

Market orders refer to orders to buy or sell stocks at their current market prices for immediate execution. If you remember from earlier, these refer to buying up at the best current ask price or selling down at the best bid price.

Depending on market conditions and subsequent price movements during the day, market orders may be the worst or best prices to trade in. For example, if you send a market order to sell when the bid-ask prices are $1.00-$1.05 and the by the time your order hits the market, the bid-ask prices shift to $0.95-$1.01, your sell order will be done at $0.95. In this example, your sell proceeds get cut by a minimum of five cents multiplied by the number of shares you sold.

On the other hand, let's say you sent a buy market order when the current bid-ask prices are $1.10-$1.15. If the bid-ask prices change to $1.12-$1.17

by the time your market order reaches the market, you'll end up paying $0.02 cents more for every share of that stock.

Only market makers and professional traders with a lot of day trading expertise and experience can benefit from market orders. For retail day traders like you and me, we should avoid market orders as much as possible. Why?

Stock Pick Scanners and Watchlists

Because there are thousands of stocks that are eligible for day trading every single trading day, it's impossible to manually scan the market for SIPs fast enough to make timely day trades. That's why you'll need to use market-scanning software to short list your day trading choices.

CHAPTER – 6
Strategies

Strategies are especially important to win at day trading. You will need to develop strategies that can be utilized over and over again so that you can continuously build a profitable portfolio. Below I have included several diverse ways to incorporate strategies into your day trading program.

Having momentum is day trading's all about. The first thing I learned when I started to trade stocks is I learned that locating stocks that are moving in price will be how you can begin to profit. Every single day, there are stocks that will move in price by 20-30% and sometimes, even more, depending on the day. So how do you identify the stocks that are fixing to make moves that could be big? One of the biggest realizations that come from day trading is that those stocks that move 20-30% of the shares will have limited technical indicators.

In order to have a momentum stock trading strategy, you will need stocks that are moving. If the stock is sideways or chopping, then it will be useless. Locating the stocks that are fixing to make a huge move is the first step. Using stock scanners to locate these is the first thing that you can do.

Momentum stocks will have a few things that are similar. By scanning 5,000 stocks you can ask for the criteria that are true to what you need. There should be a listing of at least 10 stocks per day. These will contain the ones that have a 20-30% move. These stocks will help you make a living as a day trader.

Criteria #1 - under 100mil shares that float.

Criteria #2 - charts daily that are strong.

Criteria #3 - at least 2x the volume for a volume that is high.

Criteria #4 - catalysts that are fundamental such as PR, FDA announcements, Earnings, Investor activist as well as other kinds of news that is breaking. These stocks may also experience some momentum with a catalyst fundamental. If this happens then it is going to be called a breakout technical.

Using scanners to locate my stocks for day trading is an effective way to find the ones with the criteria you need. The scanners are more valuable as a tool that many of the new traders understand.

Once the scanners pick up something, it will get alerted to that stock. Then you will have to review the candlestick chart in order to gain entry on the back pull first. Most investors will find that they need to buy this spot as well. These buyers then subsequently create spikes with the volume and subsequent results that are priced for quick sales as well as helping the stock move up. You should learn as a new trader to find an entry that shows in real time. Scanners are able to give advice for copious amounts of trade alerts on a daily basis. Instead of flipping continuously through charts, I am able to see the charts I need in a quicker more relatable way. Every trader needs to be using the scanners to find hot stocks that will help them profit daily.

Blue flags are a wonderful way to chart patterns. This is a pattern that is seen every single day during the day trading hours. It can offer a risk of entry that is low in a stock that is strong. The hardest thing is that the traders have difficulty locating these patterns in real-time. You can locate these stocks by scanning them in the scanners. If I use the surging up scanner, I can find the highest volume relative to the market. By reviewing the scanners, I can alert to the strong stocks that I will identify at a given time of day. Pattern-based traders will look for all the patterns in the stocks that will support the momentum that is continued over time. Scanners will not be able to chart the patterns that they find. This is what you will need to help with. Maintain skills to justify each trade.

Momentum Trading

The investor jumps on the stock that has a moving price that is going up. Look for these things to use this strategy:

- Prices that move in a unique and major way. Driven by earnings growth and surprise catalysts. The new launch for a drug company. Buyouts of smaller companies by larger ones.

- Movement of 30-40% in the stocks.

- A reduced number of shares that are outstanding can be traded faster by smaller stocks.

- Tools like StockTwits used for trading to maintain the momentum through ideas and trends with a platform for communications that are financial.

Bull Flags #1 Strategy

With this strategy, the first candle would be to make the high anew once the breakout happens. Now scan for the stocks and begin to squeeze up so that the green candles in the chart of the bull flag. Then the investor will wait for 2-3 candles that are red to pullback with a form. The very first candle that is green needs to make a new high once the pullback entry is at the stop that is low. This will typically show a spike in volume in the moment of the first candle that is making a high. This means that 10s of 1000s of traders are positioning themselves to take and send an order for a buy.

Flat Top Breakout #2 Strategy

This is similar to the bull flag strategy; the only difference is the pullback which is a flat top that has a strong resistant level. This will happen over a period so candles that are easy to recognize within the chart by the pattern that is obviously a flat top. This is a pattern that will form due to a big seller that has a specific level of price that can require the investors to purchase all available shares prior to the prices going higher for a continuous time. This pattern can have breakouts that are explosive for the seller's short notice which is resistant forming levels that will place a stop order right above them. If the buyer takes out the level of resistance, it can be a stop order buy which will trigger the stock to shoot a very quick high and the longs can be a nice profit if it does.

Momentum Stocks and Where to Set My Stops

I tend to set a stop order that is tight when I buy momentum stocks. This stop order is placed just below the back pull that is the first. If this stop is farther away than the 20 cents away, then you may need to place the stop order less than 20 cents and return later for a second try. The reason for the stop at 20 cents is for the 2:1 ratio of profit loss. Lastly, I risk 20 cents due to the potential to make double.

When you risk 50 or more you will need to make 1.00 to get a ratio of profit loss properly. This will make the trade justified. Try to avoid trades that would generate profits that are large for a trade that is justified. You will have a better chance of achieving a more successful trade for a stop of 20 cents and target at 40 cents vs. the 11.00 stop and the target of 2.00 profits.

Try to balance the risk across any and all trades made. When calculating risk, you will see an entry price at your stop for a look at the distance. If your stop is 20 cent and you want to max the risk, keep it at $500 and take it to 2500 shares (2500x.20=500)

Time of Day This Works Best

This is best used at the hours of 9:30-4 PM. The morning is one of the best times to trade. So, as we discussed focus on the 9:30-11:30 time period, this does not mean that any time during the day we are not able to get a news spike that should suddenly bring about amounts of volume that is tremendous in stock. This stock will have shown no interest early and then becomes a great candidate for the pullback first. This pullback that is first will be a bull flag. Once 11:30 AM arrives then the only trade-off that is done is the 5-minute chart. This is because the 1-minute chart has become choppy in what are midday as well as a trading hour through to the afternoon.

Checklist for Entry

Criteria entry #1

Momentum trading chart day pattern

Criteria Entry #2

The tight stop will support the 2:1 ratio of profit loss.

Criteria Entry #3

Volume is high, 2x or more, and associated with the catalyst. The volume getting heavier means that people tend to watch it.

Criteria Entry #4

Under 100mil shares, the float is low, however, under the 20mil share that is ideal.

Indicators for Exits

Indicator exits #1

Sell ½ when the target profit first hits. I risk $100 with hopes to make $200. Once the $200 is up, I sell ½. Then I adjust the stop for my price entry with the position of balance.

Indicators Exit #2

At the point that I have not sold ½, the candle that is first to close red is the indicator for the exit. If ½ is sold, I'll hold the candle that is red until my stop breakeven has not hit.

Indicator exit #3

The bar for extension will force me to lock at the beginning of my profits prior to the reversal inevitably begins. Bar extension is a candle that spikes up and then instantly places me up by $2-400 or more. When I have a spike in the stock, I get lucky and sell into it.

Analyze These Results

A successful trader will have metrics that are positive for their trades. Trading in stock is a statistical career. You will either have a return/ loss that generates the statistics. When working with investors, the ratio for profit and loss and their success percentage is reviewed on a regular basis. By these statistics, they will be able to see if the commitment is there or profitability has potential. This can be done without looking into their P/L total. After you have finished every week you will need to analyze results that help you with your current metrics for trading, to understand the strategies needed.

The investors that are keeping a meticulous record for trades are the best because they are data mining the records that help you understand how they can improve their trading. Using a monitoring system, you are able to follow your stats for trading and this can be a huge help when tuning your strategies into a fine plan.

There are several strategies for trading that can be used similarly to the one listed above. Below is a breakdown of each one of the trading strategies that I have found will work for day trading.

CHAPTER - 7

Steps to Success on Trading

A higher percentage of individuals fail in day trading because of ignoring crucial steps. If you have made up your mind to do day trading, there are specific steps that you ought to follow to make huge profits.

Have a trading plan.

A trading plan is a set of guidelines that need to be followed by most traders to guide them in their activities. A trading plan helps you in proper money management to avoid losses. Before executing a trading plan, you need to backtest and ensure it has positive results. Most of the trading brokers provide backtesting tools in their software. A working and an affirmative trading plan will guide you on how to do your things the right way for you to succeed.

Set an entry and exit price.

To survive in this game, you ought to have knowledge of the entry plus that of exit prices. Day trading, like any other business, has worst-case scenarios. The entry price will help you understand when to get in while the exit point will help you to know when to get out. With the prices, you will able to plan yourself on how to handle things in terms of market disasters with no worries.

Do not rush to trade when the market opens.

Have a schedule for your trading. Do not rush to trade immediately when the market opens. These are risky moments since the trades might be of the nights, and the market is not stable at that moment. You should know the best time to make your trade. Different market securities have a different time to trade. Do not be overexcited and do things anyhow. Have a timing plan for your trades.

Have limit orders.

You are highly recommended to use limit orders in trading. What is a limit order? It is a trading order which gives you the capability to make sales and purchases in market trade at a specific price. Limit orders, unlike market orders, enable you to be in control of the maximum price you will pay for and also the minimum amount you will sell. A market order allows traders to purchase or sell orders at the current prices in the market.

A market order usually is concerned with the execution of the order made rather than the price. It will execute the order so fast with the current market price, unlike a limit order. A limit order checks on the amount and makes sure it is within the parameters of the limit order. If it does not fit within the settings, no trade executions will take place.

Shun from losses.

Losses usually are part of the game in all businesses but try your best to avoid them. Small losses are sometimes not a big deal, but watch out the losses not to be continuous. You might fail terribly. Be disciplined enough and follow your trading plan strictly. Learn the mistakes you make that lead to failures and correct them.

If the losses are still there, yet you followed your trading plan, change your strategies as quickly as possible or get out of trading. To be successful in trading, you need to cut off losses which will lower your profits.

Accept losses.

Losing in trading is part of learning. Do not panic when losses occur in trading; accept them. Learn from the failures and find a solution. Do not despair or anything. Even pro traders experienced losses once or twice and worked things out.

Take advantage of technology.

Day trading is all about competition. You should choose methods or techniques that are efficient for an excellent performance. You can implement some of the means by the use of modern technology tools in trading. The technology tools may include simple charting platforms and backtesting tools.

Most of the charting platforms have simple user interface features that make it easier to read prices on the market. Backtesting tools furthermore help traders to test their trading plans and strategies for better performance in trading. Technology speeds up trading transactions and enables you to stay up to date. Staying up to date keeps you alert on any changes in the market like price fluctuations.

Be focused.

Being a focused and self-disciplined trader will save you from lots of trouble. If you want to be successful, get yourself together, have strategies and plans on how to do trading. Know when is the right time to make trades so as not to miss the golden time to make your trades. Having a schedule will keep you organized and managed. You have to follow this rule for success in day trading.

Trade with money you can afford to lose.

The risks involved in day trading are huge. The money to be used for day trading should not be capital or your savings which are essential aspects in all businesses. You should instead trade along with cash specifically for trading, which will not be a big deal when you lose it and you can recover it so fast. Do not ever think of trading with your child school fees, you will be all messed up.

Manage your risks.

You need to have ways on how to handle your trading risks. Do not ignore them or else you want to be a failure in trading. Be familiar with the dangers or your day trading will be out of control. Make trades according to the trading plan and strategies, and you will ace it.

Have a mindset of steady growth.

You should possess a mindset of steady growth in day trading. Most of the traders have the mentality of getting higher profits all at once after starting day trading. Rushing for huge benefits when you are not even stable will give you lots of stress. Relax; everything will work out well with time. Do the right thing at the right speed, and everything will eventually work out.

Avoid using margins.

Margins enable you to leverage your funds and even extra cash that you borrow from brokers. It can also increase your borrowing power. Operating on margins is sometimes risky in trading. Margins can increase or decrease in the market. The significant risk involved in margins is its big loss that occurs when the margin falls. It makes it worse when you lose the funds that you have borrowed.

Have big goals.

You need to have stringent goals for yourself. Goals will assist you in working towards something that you need to accomplish. Visualize your goals so good and perform day trading towards them. Work hard and you will succeed in day trading.

Bear the business kind of mindset.

Businesses are involved with pretty much of things. They include profits, losses, expenses, risks, stress and so much more. Normally, it is highly recommended that that in-depth research about your business has to be undertaken and good strategies have to be laid so as to improve the potential of the business. Well, this is much similar to day trading, lay out a good plan with set strategies and learn more about your day to day trading occurrences in a bid to excel and acquire large chunks of profits.

A student of the markets.

Trading markets are quite dynamic. As a trader, you ought to discover what actually used to happen, what is happening and master all the facts involved in day trading as much as possible. This makes you really informed, educated and improves your rates of managing risks. With all these outcomes, undertaking day trading becomes quite easier and chances of incurring day to day losses become limited.

Developing and implementing the trading methodology.

A day trading methodology is a system of methods that are laid down so as the trader can implement them in their day to day trading activities. This discourages hesitation that is mostly experienced by most traders that just try out their luck during trading without any plan and really expect the best out of it. Day trading is not a "get rich overnight" kind of engagement but a certain activity that calls for intelligence and several tactical skills.

Frequently using stop losses.

A stop loss is basically a predetermined amount of risk that a day trader is willing to accept with each trade. It is normally in the form of a particular percentage or a certain trading amount that limits the trader from exposure during trading. Most importantly, using stop losses ensure that risks and losses are limited.

Knowing when to stop trading.

There exist two reasons why you should most probably stop trading; the presence of an ineffective trading plan and an ineffective day trader. Major amounts of losses are expected in an ineffective trading plan probably due to the fact that markets may have changed, market volatility may have much lessened or perhaps the trading plan is just not working out as expected. This does not necessarily imply that trading has to be terminated, but the fact that a new trading plan had to be laid and strong trading strategies set.

On the other hand, an ineffective day trader is an unwanted day trader. So as to excel in day trading, there has to be a rule; be disciplined, follow your big plan, work hard and learn, be patient and so much on. If this does not entirely define you, then the chances are that day trading is not really your kind of engagement.

Keep trading in perspective.

It is advisable to focus on the bigger picture during trading. Setting realistic goals is one of the ways of keeping trading in perspective. For instance, if a trader happens to have a smaller trading account, he or she should not expect some huge returns. Always work with what you have on your plate and really try to remain sensible. It is a step to step income-generating engagement that requires much patience and a variety of day trading skills. Also, winning and losing in day trading is really going to be such common events. When winning, enjoy and celebrate your good efforts but do not lose too much control and during the sad moments, remember that losing trade is not afar off. Stay put and focused.

Trading is not entertainment.

The word has been clearly misunderstood by most traders, especially beginners. The novice should realize that day trading is an income-generating engagement and also a capital diminishing kind of activity. Remember that failing to plan is also planning to fail. Plan your strategies, learn and get your day trading journey shining all the way with just a little loss occurrence.

Learn to trade options.

With trading options, a trader has to wait for a single day before money settles after a trade. The day trading options rules are T + 1. Read several blogs describing these and most preferably, check the kind that is not really advanced to avoid making it hard to implement several kinds of strategies at the early day trading stages.

CHAPTER - 8
Rules of Day Trading

Let us turn our focus to some of the rules of day trading that every investor should follow. These rules are not necessarily set in stone. You can decide to take these rules with you on your investing journey or ignore them. However, they should be followed in order to give you the best day trading experience from the very first day of your investing career.

Day Trading is a Serious Business

When some people start day trading, they think that it is meant to be fun and games and do not take the profession seriously. This can be a grave mistake. While you want to enjoy what you are doing, you always want to remember that it is a serious business.

There are some types of investing that are easier to handle as a side career or on the weekends. If this is the type of investing, you are looking for; you will not want to look at day trading. This type of investing is meant to be a daily business and many people look at it as their day job. This means that once you decide to become a day trader officially, you need to treat it as you would any other career. You must get up in the morning, get ready for your day, and make sure you are ready to work by your set time, which could be as early as 7 in the morning.

While you will have some flexibility in your schedule from a regular job, meaning you could set a bit of a later start time in the morning, you will want to make sure to set a schedule you will follow at least Monday through Friday. Even working from home, you will want to make sure to limit distractions. For example, you will not want to focus on day trading and watching television at the same time. Set up an office for yourself and pay attention to your work. Get ready for your job as a day trader like you would for your job at any other office. Do not head into your office, in your pajamas. You are more likely to feel like you want to put in 100% effort and succeed if you treat this as a career.

Day Trading Will Not Help You Get Rich Quickly

You should not look at day trading as a get rich quick arrangement. This is a common misconception, and one reason people often turn to day trading. If you truly want to become a successful day trader, you will need to make sure you not only have the patience to build your investments, but also realize it takes time.

Day Trader is harder than it looks

Day trading is not as easy as it looks, but this does not mean that you should set this book down and decide not to become a day trader. It just means that you will probably need to spend more time learning about day trading than you initially thought. You want to make sure you are well-versed in the field before you make your first investment. Luckily for you, this is one of the reasons I decided to write this book. I want to give you a comprehensive beginner's guide so you can learn as much as you can about day trading to start your journey in one location. In other words, I have done most of the research for you.

Trading is Different from Investing

One of the biggest rules that you should understand before becoming a day trader is this is different from investing. In order to help you understand the difference, here are a few basic differences between trading and investing:

As an investor, you need to have an idea where the stocks are heading in the future. However, as a day trader, you only need to concern yourself with which stocks will give you the best financial gain on that day. You look more closely at the minutes. In fact, you will not even pay much attention to the hours and will not worry about the next day, week, month, or year.

You Will Not Win Every Trade

It does not matter how experienced you become as a day trader, there will still be days that you lose on a trade. Many people create an image in their minds where they will become so experienced at trading that they will never make a mistake and they will only gain capital.

Every game has its rules and regulations, and day trading is not any different. In case you are new to the game, you must bear in mind the entire standard rules that have been put in place to control the game. That being said, it is important to note that these rules not unbreakable, but they can be instrumental in making decisions in regard to day trading.

There are numerous rules of day trading that you have to familiarize yourself with irrespective of whether you specialize in forex, stocks, options, cryptocurrency, or futures. If you fail to abide by some of the rules, it can result in significant losses.

In as much as some rules differ depending on where you are located as well as the size of your trade, this chapter will focus on the most important rules. In addition, it will equally discuss the rules that novices can put into practice as they venture into the complicated field of day trading. These rules will also aid the experienced traders to improve their performance in trade, for instance, in the area of risk management.

Rules for Beginners

If you are new in this field, the rules of day trading that have been discussed below can help you harvest commendable profits and avoid incurring significant losses.

Get In, Exit and Escape

One major mistake that beginners make is jumping into the arena without a well thought out game plan. Do not dare to press the "enter" button if you do not have a plan of how to get in and exit. It is understandable that some elements of excitement can set in when you are new in the field. However, it is important to note that if you do not have a formidable plan, you will be thrown out of the game completely. Make use of the rules of risk management as well as stop-losses cut down losses.

Timing

I bet you usually wake up early and bright, ready to face the day ahead in the day trading arena. However, avoiding the first quarter-hour when the market is opened is arguably one of the most crucial trading rules to abide by. Most of the activity that takes place at this time involves market orders or panic trades from the previous night. You should instead use this period to follow up on reversals. The most experienced day traders also avoid the first quarter-hour.

Be Conscious of Margin

Do you remember the days when you started off, and you were looking for capital? It was very easy to fall for a margin. However, you should keep in mind that it is a loan. A loan that needs to be repaid. In as much as it can greatly revamp your profits, it also has the ability to leave you nursing significant losses. Therefore, it is advisable to learn how to trade accordingly before resorting to the margin.

Demo Accounts

You have a lot to learn and absolutely nothing to lose by taking the initiative to first practice using a demo account. You can nurture your craft with a lot of time and space for trial and error because you are being funded by money that has been simulated. Very many brokers will give you free accounts so that you can practice because they are the best place to learn about strategies, patterns, and charts, as well as the quarter-hour day trading practice.

Learn to Accept the Loss

Virtually all the veteran traders have all achieved what they have achieved because they were willing to lose and learn from it. Losing is just the pathway to get more experience, embrace it.

That being said, it is also important to say that cutting down your losses is very important.

Take in Everything

One veteran once said that a great trader is similar to an athlete, he might possess, but he has to train himself on how to use them. Complacency should not be something that great traders relate to because they should always be; I am searching for that edge. This means that they resort to a wide range of resources to boost their knowledge. They can use anything, ranging from videos, books, blogs, and forums.

Do an Evaluation of Tips

It is normal to get excited when you are given a tip that is thought-provoking. Nonetheless, unconfirmed tips from relatively undependable sources can result in significant losses. Jesse Livermore, a trader, said that experience had taught him a tip or a number of tips that will make him more money than what his judgment can. Therefore, ensure that you double-check any information that may affect your decisions as a trader.

Rules of Risk Management

The rules of money management and the risks of day trading are key determinants of how prosperous a trader will be. In as much as you do not have to follow these rules to the letter, they have proven to be indispensable to many.

1% Risk Rule

Here, the idea is to bar you from trading beyond your ability. When you put this technique into use irrespective of whether a trade subsidy or not, you will always have some reserve I am stacked in the bank to help you correct your balance later on.

The idea is that you should never engage in trade with more than 1% of your total account on one trade. For example, if your account has $50,000, you will only use up to $500 on your trade.

Why Use It?

You will have to lose over 100 trades simultaneously to clear your bank account balance completely. This is important to safeguard your earnings when market conditions are volatile as you get good returns in the process.

I bet you are worried that you will not be raking in maximum profits if you trade so meagerly. Calm down. You can make good profits. If you stake 1%, you should expect a profit of about 1.5%—2%. If you trade several times a day, the profits will definitely make themselves evident.

It is arguably the best approach for the people that are starting off. In as much as you get to experience through trial and error, losses can come fast and thick. However, if you are consistent, it will teach you the tricks of the game until you become a veteran in trading with an arsenal of techniques for making maximum profits in daily training.

Variations

As soon as you have created an efficient technique, you can make changes to your risk tolerance. You can upgrade it to 1.5% or 2%. However, it is important to note that traders with $100,000 in their accounts should not risk more than 1% in one trade because even a 1% loss could have a massive impact.

Basically, it is about finding an area that you and comfortable with, and it also connects with your style of trade.

CHAPTER - 9
Beginners Traders

Building Up Your Watch List

The first step when you are ready to get started in day trading is to do some research. When you first wake up in the morning, look over your notes and your research and then use that information to create a good watch list. This watch list can be important because it can limit you down to just a few options that you plan to use for trading on that day. There are thousands of stocks on the market and making this watch list will make it so much easier for you to pick the right stocks to invest in.

There are different methods you can use to create this watch list. But one of the best options is to use a scanner. These scanners can look for specific criteria that you want out of stock and can make things faster than trying to look through them all on your own. To make the scanner work, you just need to list out the requirements that you want the stock to meet and then the scanner will alert you as soon as it finds one that meets these.

Decide Which of These Stocks Work Best For You

After the scanner has given you a few options for stocks that meet your requirements, you can decide which of these the best stocks are. You may have a specific strategy that you would like to go with and then choose the stock that seems to be following that strategy the best. You can always change strategies from one day to the next, or you can choose to stick with one strategy if it is serving your purpose.

As we discussed in some of our strategies before, make sure that you do not trade in the market for at least the first five minutes after the market opens. Some professionals wait even longer than these five minutes for the market to settle down. There can be a ton of commotion and crazy ups and downs in the market during those first few minutes and investing at this time can hurt your profits. If you spend time looking at your scanner and then investigating the stocks that you receive, it will probably be at least five or more minutes before you are ready to enter the market anyway, but it is still important to be aware of this volatility and learn how to avoid it.

Put That Entry and Exit Strategy in Place

Now that you have a few stocks that are ready to go, you're probably excited to get into the market and start doing you is trading. Before you make that purchase, you need to finish up your strategies. This isn't just the overall strategy but also the center and the exit strategy so you know how to get into and out of the market at the right times.

The first strategy you should work with here is your entry strategy. This is the place where you are comfortable and will purchase your stock. Your aim is to get this entry point as low as you can so that you don't spend too much money and to increase your profits later on. When you look through the charts for that stock, you should be able to figure out a safe entry point that will provide you with a reasonable price on that stock.

You also need to come up with an exit strategy. It is important to have a stop for losing money and one for earning money. First, let's look at the stop to losing money. There are times when the strategies that you pick or the decisions that you make are not going to turn out how you wanted and the stock may start to lose money. The point of this stop is to ensure that you can control how much money you will lose in the process. Once the stock ends up reaching this number, you will withdraw from the market, no matter what the stock does later on.

Without this stop, you could end up with a little bit of trouble. Many new traders see that the stock is going down, and they keep riding it out. They hope that the market will turn around. Sometimes the market will turn around, but then there are times when the market will stay low or keep going down.

Purchase the Stocks You Want

After you created your watch list and came up with your enter and exit strategies to keep you safe, it is time to actually go into the market and make your purchase. You will want to have all the criteria in place for that stock before doing this. But if you are working with a strategy, that is going to outline the criteria for you, so just follow that.

If you plan to work with your broker when doing day trading, you would just give them your order to get the trade started. The order is going to include a ton of information that can help the broker do everything that you want. This would include information on which stocks, in particular, you want to purchase, how many shares of each you want to purchase, how much you will spend on these stocks, when you want to enter the market, and when you want to exit the market. The broker is then able to take that information and place the order for you in the system.

There is also the option for you to do all of the work on your own. This is fine to do but most beginner traders are not going to pick this option because they worry about messing things up or doing something wrong.

Pay Attention

You will quickly find that day trading has some differences compared to other stock trading options. Many other options are longer-term; you purchase the stock and then ride out the market, hoping that your choice will go up over some time. But with day trading, you are only letting the trade occur in one day. The purchase of the stock, as well as the sale of it, all need to happen sometime between open and close of the same day.

This does make day trading a riskier option to work with compared to some of the other stock trading options. This means that you need to really want the market and make some quick decisions on when to buy and sell your stocks. If you don't watch the market, then how are you going to be able to make these quick changes when needed?

As a day trader, you get to focus on watching these ups and downs that occur during the day. This can make it easier to know when you should purchase a stock in the first place and then it helps you to figure out when you can sell the stocks to make the biggest profits, or to keep your losses to a minimum.

Once you enter into a trade, you need to pay attention to the market and there may be times when the market changes quickly and you will need to make some quick changes to your position, or close it out, to help you earn more profits or keep the losses down as much as possible. Day trading is not one of those methods where you can place the order and then walk away. If you don't have the time to sit and closely watch the market, make sure to not place an order until you have more time.

Sell Your Stocks When They Reach Your Original Exit Points

It is a good idea to listen to your exit point not only when the market is going down but also when the market is going up. Some people understand why they should follow the exit strategy when the market is going down and they do not want to end up losing too much money in the market. It is a bit harder on them when the market is going up. They may have placed a stop for how much profit they wanted to make, but then they see the market still goes up and they do not want to get out at that time.

While it may be hard, make sure that you are listening to your exit strategy, even when the market is going up. Sure, the market may go past that point, but then it may hit a sharp downturn and you could lose all of that profit. This is another method in place to ensure that your investment stays safe. If the market continues to do well and keeps going up, you will be able to jump back in later on.

Take Some Time to Reflect on That Trade and Write Down Some of the Information as Research Later

As a beginner in the day trading world, there are a lot of things to learn about the market. This is even truer if you have never invested in the past. As a trader, it is your job to learn as you go and make some changes if it is needed. But when you are learning a lot of strategies and keeping track of a large number of trades that are done in day trading, it can be hard to remember everything over time.

Getting a journal and writing down some of your mistakes, your tips, and more after each trade can make a difference.

You don't have to write down a lot of information unless you want to. Just have a few lines or a paragraph. This may seem like it wastes your time. But if you ever get stuck on a trade later on, or if you are trying to figure out why you are in a slump and not getting the profits that you want, looking back through this information can make a big difference in how things go in the future.

Startup Your Second (And Third and Fourth and So On) Trade

Day trading moves very fast. It is likely that your first trade can be made in a few minutes, though as a beginner it will probably take a little bit longer to finish. If there is still time left in the day when you finish up that first trade, then go through these steps again and complete the next trade. Day traders earn a big profit simply by making a bunch of little trades.

The more of these successful trades that you can get into one day, the more profit you will make. Just make sure that you are following the same steps that we talked about above and take the same precautions that you did with your first trade. If there is not enough time during the day, or you worry that you will rush yourself if you try to make another trade, it is fine to take a break and resume the next day.

There are times when you are going to get into the day trading market and you will make a bad trade in the morning. It may

Not have gone your way, you may have tried to switch your strategy partway through, or maybe you let your emotions get in the way. If the trade was really bad and you feel upset about it, then it is best to just call it good and take a step away from the market for the rest of the day.

CHAPTER - 10

Huge Mistakes That Beginners Make

Aside from doing the right things, you'll also need to refrain from certain things to succeed as a day trader. Here are some of the most common day trading mistakes you should avoid committing.

Excessive Day Trading

By excessive, I mean executing too many day trades. One of the most common mistakes many newbie day traders make is assuming that they can become day trading ninjas in just a couple of weeks if they trade often enough to get it right. But while more practice can eventually translate into day trading mastery later on, it doesn't mean you can cram all that practice in a very short period of time via very frequent day trading. The adage "the more, the merrier" doesn't necessarily apply to day trading.

Remember, timing is crucial for day trading success. And timing is dependent on how the market is doing during the day. There will be days when day trading opportunities are few and far between and there'll be days when day trading opportunities abound. Don't force trades for the sake of getting enough day trades under your belt.

Even in the midst of a plethora of profitable day trading opportunities, the more the merrier still doesn't apply. Why? If you're a newbie trader, your best bet at becoming a day trading ninja at the soonest possible time is to concentrate on one or two day trades per day only. By limiting your day trades, to just one or two, you have the opportunity to closely monitor and learn from your trades.

Can you imagine executing 5 or more trades daily as a newbie and monitor all those positions simultaneously? You'll only get confused and overwhelmed and worse, you may even Miss Day trading triggers and signals and fail to profitably close your positions.

Winging It

If you want to succeed as a day trader, you need to hold each trading day in reverence and high esteem. How do you do that? By planning your day trading strategies for the day and executing those strategies instead of just winging it.

As cliché as it may sound, failing to plan really is planning to fail. And considering the financial stakes involved in day trading, you shouldn't go through your trading days without any plan on hand. Luck favors those who are prepared and planning can convince lady luck that you are prepared.

Expecting Too Much Too Soon

This much is true about day trading: it's one of the most exciting and exhilarating jobs in the world! And stories many day traders tell of riches accumulated through this economic activity add more excitement, desire, and urgency for many to get into it.

However, too much excitement and desire resulting from many day trading success stories can be very detrimental to newbie day traders. Let me correct myself: it is detrimental to newbie day traders. Why?

Such stories, many of which are probably urban legends, give newbies unrealistic expectations of quick and easy day trading riches. Many beginner day traders get the impression that day trading is a get-rich-quick scheme!

It's not. What many day traders hardly brag about are the times they also lost money and how long it took them to master the craft enough to quit their jobs and do it full time. And even rarer are stories of the myriad number of people who've attempted day trading and failed. It's the dearth of such stories that tend to make day trading neophytes have unrealistic expectations about day trading.

What's the problem with lofty day trading expectations? Here's the problem: if you have very unrealistic expectations, it's almost certain that you'll fail. It's because unrealistic expectations can't be met and therefore, there are zero chances for success.

One of the most unrealistic expectations surrounding day trading is being able to double one's initial trading capital in a couple of months, at most. Similar to such expectations is that of being able to quit one's day job and live an abundant life in just a few months via day trading. Successful day traders went through numerous failures, too, before they succeeded at day trading and were able to do it for a living.

Changing Strategies Frequently

Do you know how to ride a bike? If not, do you know someone who does? Whether it's you or somebody you know, learning how to ride a bike wasn't instant. It took time and a couple of falls and bruises along the way.

But despite falls, scratches and bruises, you or that person you know stuck to learning how to ride a bike and with enough time and practice, succeeded in doing so. It was because you or the other person knew that initial failures mean that riding a bike was impossible. It's just challenging at first.

It's the same with learning how to day trade profitably. You'll need to give yourself enough time and practice to master it. Just because you suffered trading losses in the beginning doesn't mean it's not working or it's not for you. It probably means you haven't really mastered it yet.

But if you quit and shift to a new trading strategy or plan quickly, you'll have to start again from scratch, extend your learning time, and possibly lose more money than you would've if you stuck around to your initial strategy long enough to give yourself a shot at day trading successfully or concluding with certainty that it's not working for you.

If you frequently change your day trading strategies, i.e., you don't give yourself enough time to learn day trading strategies, your chances of mastering them become much lower. In which case, your chances of succeeding in day trading become much lower, too.

Not Analyzing Past Trades

Those who don't learn history are doomed to repeat it, said writer and philosopher George Santayana. We can paraphrase it to apply to day traders, too: Those who don't learn from their day trading mistakes will be doomed to repeat them.

If you don't keep a day trading journal containing records of all your trades and more importantly, analyze them, you'll be doomed to repeat your losing day trades. It's because by not doing so, you won't be able to determine what you're doing wrong and what you should be doing instead in order to have more profitable day trades than losing ones.

Ditching Correlations

We can define correlations as a relationship where one thing influences the outcome or behavior of another. A positive correlation means that both tend to move in the same direction or exhibit similar behaviors, i.e., when one goes up, the other goes up, too, and vice versa.

Correlations abound in the stock market. For example, returns on the stock market are usually negatively correlated with the Federal Reserve's interest rates, i.e., when the Feds increase interest rates, returns on stock market investments go down and vice versa.

Correlations exist across industries in the stock market, too. For example, property development stocks are positively correlated to steel and cement manufacturing stocks. This is because when the property development's booming, it buys more steel and cement from manufacturing companies, which in turn also increase their income.

Ignoring correlations during day trading increases your risks for erroneous position taking and exiting. You may take a short position on a steel manufacturer's stock while taking a long position on a property development company's stock and if they have a positive correlation, one of those two positions will most likely end up in a loss.

But caution must be exercised with using correlations in your day trades. Don't establish correlations where there's none. Your job is to simply identify if there are observable correlations, what those correlations are, and how strong they are.

Being Greedy

Sadly for the owner, there were no golden eggs inside the goose because it only created and laid one golden egg every day. His greed caused him to destroy his only wealth-generating asset.

When it comes to day trading, greed can have the same negative financial impact. Greed can make a day trader hold on to an already profitable position longer than needed and result in smaller profits later on or worse, trading losses.

If you remember my story, that was greed in action. Had I been content with the very good returns I already had and closed my position, my paper gains could've become actual gains. I let my greed control my trading and chose to hold on to that stock much longer than I needed to. That trade turned into a losing one eventually.

That's why you must be disciplined enough to stick to your day trading stop-loss and profit-taking limits. And that's why you should program those limits on your platform, too. Doing so minimizes the risks of greed hijacking your otherwise profitable day trades.

CHAPTER – 11

Tips for Day Trading In Options

Day trading in options can be a new experience for a lot of traders. They may not be ready to take on all the challenges that come with it and mixing these two different strategies and securities together can make for some interesting trades on the market. Some of the tips that you can use to see better results with day trading in options include:

Using Software for Your Trades

There are some software programs available that can make your work easier with day trading options. These will allow you to put in some of the requirements that you want for a trade, such as the amount of volatility, the amount you want to spend on each trade, the entry and exit points, and more, and then they will search for the right securities to use. They can do the trading for you and help you to earn money as you learn the system.

This doesn't mean that you should set these up and then walk away. In fact, this could be a very bad way to handle it. The software programs are not perfect, and you won't learn anything about the market if you let them do every bit of the work. You should still be an active participant, even if you are utilizing these services. With that said, you may find that they can teach you more about the market, can help you find trades where you may have missed them, and can lower the risk that you experience as a trader.

Never Invest More Than You Can Afford To Lose

It can be tempting to invest more than your initial amount. You may have put money into savings and agreed that this was the only amount that you would spend on the trades. And you had meant to stay with it. But then a good trade comes in, and you think that you just need to put a little bit more down to really see the results.

The promise with this is that once you start putting down more money than you can afford to lose on a trade, you are increasing your risks. Always assume that you are going to lose on a trade, and then do what you can to prevent this from happening. There are going to be some trades that don't go well for you, no matter how hard you try or how convincing the signs were. If you follow this tip, and the trade does go south, then you are only losing money that had been set aside for this purpose anyway, and you won't be scrambling to pay other things off.

Be Careful When Someone Tries To Sell a Certain Security

You want to be making your own decisions when it comes to day trading or any kind of investment for that matter. You must do your research and pick out the trading strategy that you are the most comfortable with. This is the only way that you will see the results that you want when you start trading.

As a beginner, there are always going to be people out there who will try to convince you to go after one security over another, or to try some new system or another. While some of these individuals may be offering you some good advice, you should always consider the reason behind why they want you to invest with a particular security over another.

In many cases, the individual or group who is trying to talk you into one security of another, and they often add in a ton of pressure and persuasion as well, is the one who is going to profit from this trade. They may make a commission on getting people to buy in or are rewarded in other ways. They don't really care what happens to you when you trade on that security, they just want to be the ones to make money, and often this can harm your capital and your own investment.

Consequently you always need to do your own research when you start out with investing. There are plenty of resources that you can use, lots of charts, and even many people you can talk to. But regardless of what others tell you to do or not do, you must make many of these decisions on your own to help ensure they are the right ones for you.

Do Not Trade On the Margin

As you get into trading, you may start to hear about something that is known as trading on the margin. This is an option that is available through some brokers, and it can allow you to have more purchasing power on the market, with less money down on your part. But it is very risky, and it is not really a good idea to work with this in day trading, especially if you are a beginner.

What this basically consists of is a loan from the broker. You may put in $7,000 for a trade, and then they loan you $15,000 (or some other amount so that you can now put in $22,000 on that trade. There will be fees and other costs that come with this loan. And you will owe on it whether the trade turns out in your favor, or not.

If you end up having a trade that works in your favor, then you will be able to pay back the amount that you owe the broker, along with pocketing some of the profits. But if the trade goes poorly, not only did you lose the $7000 that you invested of your own money, but you also lost the additional

$15,000 that the broker loaned you, along with any fees and other costs that are assessed on that money.

As you can see, the amount of loss is now much larger. While this method could potentially bring you some more profits, it can be a dangerous game to play in this market. It is much better to only invest the amount of money that you are comfortable with losing, and that you already have in your personal possession, rather than trying to play on the margin and risking more than you can afford.

Remember Those Entry and Exit Points

We talked about these a bit before, but it is always a good idea to set up your entry and exit points. In fact, before you ever think about entering a trade, make sure to look at the charts and determine the best entry and exit points possible. These help ensure that you are going to make the highest potential profits possible, and can keep your risks down to a minimum.

As a new investor, you are probably excited to get started and join the market. You will find that this energy is going to help you get far when it comes to your investing goals. However, if you don't slow down, at least enough to come up with logical and sound entry and exit points, then you are going to end up with a lot of trouble with all your trades. Put these entry and exit points in place before you do anything else with the trading.

Keep the Emotions At Home

Emotions are going to turn into your worst enemy when it comes to working with day trading. This is a fast-moving market, and if you get caught up in excitement, revenge, or greed (just to name a few of the possible emotions you may experience), then you are going to end up losing, rather than gaining, a lot of money with day trading.

Emotions make you forget all the trading strategies that you worked hard on and all of the research and analysis that you do. It may make you stay in a trade too long because you want to recover your losses, only to result in even more losses. Or you may stay in the trade too long when you are earning profits, and then the market reverses and you either make less in profits, or you earn nothing.

If you are someone who can't control their emotions well when the stakes are high, then day trading is probably not the answer for you. You may find long-term investing a better fit, or some other method of investing. By day trading is fast, emotional, and requires a lot of quick thinking. If you aren't able to keep up with it, then you will end up losing your profits.

Take a Break When Needed

Day trading options can be exciting, intense, and a lot of fun. There is the potential to make a lot of money on the trades, but there is also the potential to lose a lot of money on a trade. And since you need to enter and exit a trade all on the same day, it can mean a lot of time watching and analyzing the market in a short amount of time. For beginners and experts alike, day trading can end up being very exhausting and hard to keep up with.

If you find that you are having trouble keeping up with the market, or maybe you are making more mistakes than usual, then maybe it is time to consider taking a break from your trading, even for just a few days. Sometimes we just need a refresh, some time away from the trade. Then we can come back better than ever and ready to take on the best trade of our investing career.

Don't Revenge Trade

One of the worst things that you can do when you get started with day trading options is to fall into the trap of revenge trading. What this is is a tendency to try and make up for losing money when a trade goes bad. You end up losing some money, often not that much, but you are disappointed in the fact that you did lose money in the first place. As a result, you decide that it is time to earn that money back and more.

This may sound like a good idea, but in reality, you are too concentrated on showing the market who's boss and showing others how much you can make, that you aren't paying attention and you won't make sound investing decisions. In many cases, because you have given up on some of the techniques that we talked about before, and because you have allowed your emotions to take over, you will end up losing more and more money over time.

If you do end up with a bad trade, and you start to feel emotions creep in, then take a break. There is nothing wrong with just taking a few days off and doing something else. Day trading options can be very time consuming, and sometimes very intense. Taking that break can be just what you need. After a few days, you will have gotten over the loss, have cleared out your head, and will be ready to get back into the game and see some great results.

Day trading, along with other forms of investing, can be a challenge and learning all the strategies, how to read the charts and more can sometimes seem overwhelming. Then on top of that, you also want to make sure that you can reduce your risks as much as possible. If you are able to follow the steps and tips above, you will be able to reduce the amount of risk you face when you get started with day trading.

CONCLUSION

Thank you for making it through to the end of Day Trading Strategies for Beginners, I hope it was informative enough to give you the insight that is needed to make it possible for you to have the tools that you will need to achieve your goals as a day trader in the stock market.

Your next step is to sign up for an account and begin to see how much money you could be earning on any given day. If you do not have the necessary and required funds to start day trading, then I would not suggest that you do a margin since this will place you further in debt. There are several strategies in this book to help you develop one that is right for you. I have included the psychology behind day trading and what it means to fit the bill of a day trader. Over time the market can rise and fall and as a day trader you will take advantage of these market fluctuations and build a future by purchasing and then subsequently dropping the stocks that you pick up. Many people believe that day trading is fun until the stress gets to them. Make sure that you are physically and mentally fit to begin this career; otherwise you may lose more than just money. Day trading takes time and money and if you do not have any of that then it is not the right job for you.

Day Trading is a very profitable business for some but can be devastating for investors who aren't' prepared with the specific skills it requires and the high-pressure environment it creates. If you want to try your hand as a day trader you'll be up against experts who have access to mountains of information and steady hands honed by years of practice. This is not to warn you off this path, but to ensure that if this is a route you plan to go down you're prepared for success.

The brokerage fees accrued with this many trades add up, and you have to make a lot of successful trades to offset them. Make sure to factor these in when deciding whether day trades are for you. At the end of this guidebook here are the seven tips for always:

1. Don't let your emotions get the best of you.

You have a wealth of information at your fingertips, and now you have the wherewithal to turn all that info into actionable steps. Don't let prides, or wanting to be right, or fear derail you.

2. Trust Yourself

This is the key difference between an okay trader and a great one. It might seem like this contradicts the previous piece of advice, but if you've done your homework and come to a fact-based conclusion, don't let the opinions of others turn you from the path you've decided on.

3. Don't worry about what's "Hot"

This builds on Tip 2. When you get into the world of investing you'll be getting tips left and right from people who may or may not have an ulterior motive, and almost certainly won't have as much insight into your particular needs as you do. It's easy to let excitement carry you along, but it's almost always dangerous. If you're hearing that a stock is "hot" at a dinner party everyone already knows about it, and it's probably overvalued by this point.

4. Remember Context

Investing doesn't happen in a vacuum. When you hear horror stories about someone losing their house in bad trades, it's always because they forgot about the context of their life. You have to have income that pays the bills and forgetting that to chase the next big windfall is just another emotional mistake that you must avoid.

5. Never. Stop. Diversifying.

Diversification isn't a one-time process. As you sell off parts of your portfolio, you'll reinvest that money in other ways. Make sure your portfolio remains diverse.

6. Be Patient

Making money on the stock market takes a cool head and a steady hand. If you jump out of the water every time it gets a little warm you don't stand a chance. You'll take losses, but you now know how to deal with them. Don't let a small loss become a drain on your assets or on your focus.

7. Respect the Time Limitations of Your Investments

Say you invest in a fund or bond that requires you to hold it for a specified amount of time. During this time, the market spikes, and you realize you'd still make a little bit of money if you sell now and pay the fee for exiting early. While you didn't lose anything in this transaction overall, you've lost the opportunity for that money to make as much as it could have if properly invested. If you know you'll need cash to hand during the time an investment requires, pick a different investment.

So there you have it, I hope you have learned something and good luck on your day trading journey!